크롭 인 도쿄 오사카 교토 나라

1판 1쇄 발행일 2025년 6월 6일

사진 박형설 (루시안)
글　박형설 (루시안)

발행인 최진
발행처 트립풀
출판등록 2022년 9월 23일 (제 2024-000002호)
주소 경기도 화성시 남양중앙로 419
전화 010-4494-4450
홈페이지 tripfull.kr　**인스타그램** @_tripfull

편집/디자인 트립풀

ⓒ 트립풀, 2025

ISBN 979-11-984186-7-8 (03660)

값은 뒤표지에 있습니다.
이 책은 저작권법에 따라 보호받는 저작물이므로 무단 전재와 무단 복제를 금합니다.
이 책의 전부 또는 일부를 이용하려면 반드시 저자와 트립풀의 동의를 받아야 합니다.
잘못된 책은 교환해 드립니다.

CROP in TOKYO, OSAKA

ISBN 979-11-984186-7-8 (03660)

Photographed by Lucian
Written by Lucian
Retouched by Lucian

Published by Tripfull
Edited by Hong Chongchong

ⓒ 2025 Tripfull
All right reserved. No part of this publication may be reproduced, stored in a retrieval system or transmitted, in any form or by any means, electronic, mechanical, photocopying, recording or otherwise, without the written permission of the publisher and the photographer.

Osan City, Republic of KOREA
tripfull.kr
@_tripfull
tripfull@naver.com

A Whisper from the Author

Cityscapes often speak in silence, yet within that quiet, countless stories breathe. As I wandered through the narrow alleys of Tokyo, even the soft glow from an old sign seemed to hold someone's memory. In the laughter drifting across Osaka's bustling streets, I felt the warmth of life unfolding in real time. This book captures those unspoken conversations—tender moments brushed against by time. A sense of belonging in unfamiliar corners, serenity blooming in the midst of chaos, fleeting stillness at the edge of a hurried day. My camera preserved the light, and my heart translated the feeling into words. Each page in this book is a quiet fragment of the cities I met—like a kind coincidence. A dusky alley painted with crossing shadows and light, a window scene watched in stillness, a figure pausing beneath the soft hum of a vending machine. In those small moments, I found pieces of myself and stories I longed to share. In the whirlwind of everyday life, I hope this book becomes a gentle pause in your heart. These are the whispers offered to me by Tokyo and Osaka—now softly handed to you.

June, 2025
By the sunlit window facing south
Lucian

작가가 당신에게

　　도시의 풍경은 때로 말이 없지만, 그 침묵 속엔 수많은 이야기가 숨 쉽니다. 도쿄의 좁은 골목을 따라 걷다 보면, 오래된 간판 사이로 스며드는 노란 불빛 하나에도 누군가의 기억이 깃들어 있습니다. 오사카의 분주한 거리 위를 떠도는 웃음소리 속에는 살아 있는 지금의 온기도 있습니다. 이 책은 그 소리 없는 대화들과 마주한 순간들을 담았습니다. 낯선 도시에서 느낀 정겨움, 군중 속에서도 흐르던 고요한 감정, 바쁜 하루의 끝자락에서 피어난 작은 평온들. 카메라는 그 순간들을 기록했고, 마음은 그 감정들을 글로 새겼습니다. 이 책에 실린 한 장 한 장은, 다정한 우연처럼 마주한 도시의 조각들입니다. 빛과 어둠이 교차하던 저녁 골목, 말없이 바라보던 창가의 풍경, 자판기 불빛 아래 멈춰 선 한 사람의 뒷모습. 그 모든 장면 속에서 저는 저를 발견했고, 당신과 나눌 이야기를 품었습니다. 바쁘게 흘러가는 날들 속에서, 이 책이 잠시나마 당신의 마음에 조용한 쉼표가 되어주길 바랍니다. 도쿄와 오사카라는 두 도시가 건네준 속삭임을, 이제 당신에게 건네고 싶습니다.

2025년 6월,
남쪽의 볕드는 창가에서
박형설

Chapters Unfolded

CROP in TOKYO, OSAKA

DAY _____ 07

NIGHT _____ 83

목차

크롭인 도쿄 오사카 교토 나라

낮 _____ 07

밤 _____ 83

CROP in TOKYO, OSAKA

DAY

낮

On the path to the Imperial Palace, trees steeped in the breath of time, golden leaves trembling in the afternoon light. The stone walls of the moat quietly cradle the passing centuries. The wind whispers of the past, and on the mirrored surface of the water, the sky drifts by. Footsteps echo along the stone path, memories where history entwines and coexists. Sunlight shatters brilliantly through the branches, and shadows walk quietly along the way. Ginkgo leaves offer their final farewell, and the ripples bid a gentle goodbye. Serene majesty. A thousand years of whispers. Unforgettable footsteps. Even today, all things overlap along this path.

고쿄로 향하는 길, 시간의 숨결에 젖은 나무들, 황금빛 잎새가 떨리는 오후, 해자의 돌벽은 묵묵히 세월을 품고 있다. 바람은 과거를 속삭이고, 물 속 그림자 표면에는 하늘이 흐른다. 돌길 위의 발자국들, 역사가 뒤엉켜 공존한 기억, 태양은 나뭇가지 사이로 찬란하게 부서지고, 그림자는 조용히 길을 따라 걷는다. 은행잎은 마지막 인사를 건네고, 물결은 고요히 작별 인사를 고한다. 고요한 위엄. 천 년의 속삭임. 잊혀지지 않는 발걸음. 오늘도 그 길 위에 겹쳐지는 모든 것들.

MQJ6+PQJ Chiyoda City, Tokyo, Japan

#5299c9, 79,19,7,0
#9ac7e7, 49,4,4,0
#d1b332, 14,26,95,1
#3d392b, 60,57,77,64
#b99933, 20,35,95,6

Sunlight sketches itself upon the walls of a grey city. Beyond the window, a bicycle quietly dreams. Two footsteps leave echoes along the street. A crimson bag, a black coat, a checkered skirt. The wind drifts slowly, as always, through the day. A blue frame beyond the glass, time suspended. The city, indifferent, lets another day slip by. Shadows of clouds brush against the walls. Spring lingers at the toes of those who wander. A gaze pauses, then the journey resumes. In unfamiliar alleys and familiar scenes. Light and shadow walk side by side. An unnamed day, a familiar afternoon. The world beyond the window flows quietly on.

회색 도시의 벽에 햇살이 그려지고, 창 너머 자전거가 조용히 꿈을 꾼다. 두 사람의 발걸음이 길 위에 소리를 남긴다. 붉은 가방, 검은 코트, 체크무늬 치마. 바람은 오늘도 천천히 흐른다. 유리창 너머의 푸른 프레임, 멈춘 시간. 도시는 무심하게 하루를 넘긴다. 구름의 그림자가 벽을 스친다. 걷는 이들의 발끝에 봄이 머문다. 잠시 멈춘 시선, 다시 이어지는 걸음. 낯선 골목과 익숙한 풍경 속에서 빛과 그림자가 어깨를 맞댄다. 이름 모를 하루, 익숙한 오후. 창밖의 풍경은 조용히 흘러간다.

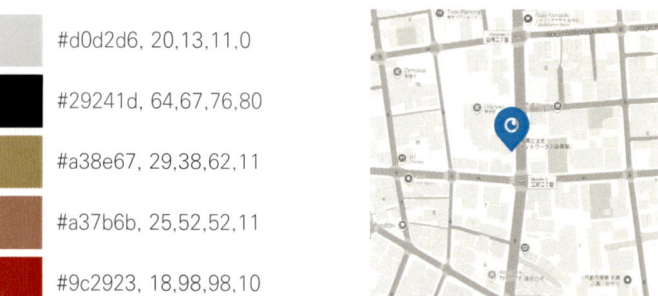

2-chōme-17 Miyoshi, Koto City, Tokyo 135-0022

#d0d2d6, 20,13,11,0
#29241d, 64,67,76,80
#a38e67, 29,38,62,11
#a37b6b, 25,52,52,11
#9c2923, 18,98,98,10

An alley cast in shadow. Silence flows through tangled wires overhead. Stillness hidden between footsteps. The heartbeat of life breathes beneath concrete. Morning light etches itself upon glass and steel. Faint silhouettes cast trembling shadows. Amid stitched solitude, towering buildings stand as silent sentinels. The low hum of a bicycle resonates with memory, stories seeping through cracks in brick. Time folds between the buildings' embrace. A fleeting moment, the rustle of a coat, footsteps wrapped in winter's hush. In narrow alleys where stories bloom, a gentle loneliness wrapped in morning light. The city's quiet dance, choreographed in geometric grace, a strange midday dream caught in tangled wires.

그림자가 드리운 골목. 얽혀있는 전깃줄 사이로 고요가 흐른다. 발자국 사이에 숨겨진 정적. 콘크리트 속에서 숨 쉬는 삶의 맥박. 어느덧 아침 햇살은 유리와 철골에 새겨진다. 그림자를 떨구는 희미한 실루엣. 햇살 속에 꿰맨 고독 속에서 파수꾼처럼 서 있는 고층 빌딩. 자전거의 낮은 울림은 기억을 공명하고, 이야기는 벽돌 틈으로 스며든다. 건물 사이 접힌 시간의 틈. 스쳐 지나가는 순간, 코트가 바스락거리고, 발자국은 겨울 정적에 싸인다. 스토리가 피어나는 좁은 골목, 아침 햇살에 부드럽게 감싸인 어떤 외로움. 기하학으로 추는 도시의 조용한 춤, 엉킨 전선 사이에 걸린 생경한 한낮의 꿈일지도.

3-chōme-6 Shirakawa, Koto City, Tokyo 135-0021

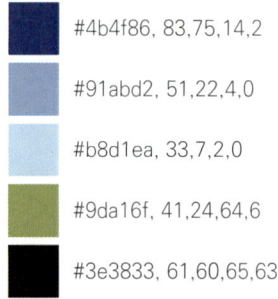

#4b4f86, 83,75,14,2

#91abd2, 51,22,4,0

#b8d1ea, 33,7,2,0

#9da16f, 41,24,64,6

#3e3833, 61,60,65,63

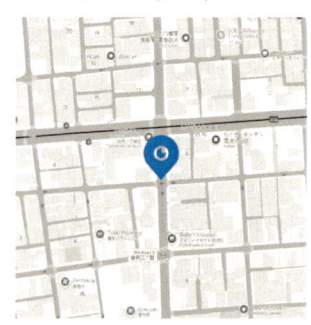

Amid the swift current of the Shinkansen, Mount Fuji emerges in majestic silhouette-a silent guardian among the endless sprawl of the city. The snow-capped peak glows with tranquil brilliance, as if time itself has paused, indifferent to the hurried lives below. In the chill of early morning sunlight, the mountain watches over the earth's breath, becoming, through centuries, a symbol of unchanging serenity and strength, quietly observing the fleeting moments of the world-an eternal witness to the transience of all things.

신칸센의 빠른 흐름 속에서, 후지산은 거대한 형상으로 떠오른다. 끝없이 펼쳐진 도시 사이에서 침묵의 수호자처럼. 설산은 마치 시간이 멈춘 듯, 아래의 빠르게 변하는 삶을 아랑곳하지 않고 고요히 빛난다. 이른 아침의 차가운 햇살 속에서, 산은 땅의 숨결을 지켜보며, 수백 년을 거쳐 변화 없는 평온과 힘의 상징이 되어, 세상의 덧없는 순간들을 조용히 관찰하고 있다.

#84897c, 49,33,47,13

#c6d2d6, 26,10,13,0

#697989, 65,42,2,11

#55799e, 78,42,19,4

#55729d, 78,48,16,3

4MXR+C6Q Fuji, Shizuoka, Japan

Silver birds, sculpted from cold metal, perch in a quiet row along the railing, basking in sunlight. White letters cast gentle shadows on black asphalt, as the breeze softly weaves between four little birds. On the guardrail between road and pavement, their forms linger gracefully in the deep contrast of fleeting motion and stillness. Distant ivy breathes in deep green, and time on the road seems to pause in tranquil silence. Warmth nestles within the chill of metal, as their silent gazes meet. Amid the city's restless flow, these birds quietly assert their presence, inviting a pause to encounter the calm within the rush.

은빛 작은 새들이 차가운 금속으로 형상화되어 난간 위에 나란히 앉아 햇살을 머금는다. 검은 아스팔트 위 하얀 글자가 조용히 그림자를 드리우고, 바람은 네 마리 새 사이를 살며시 스쳐간다. 도로와 인도 사이 가드레일 위, 세상의 흐름과 고요한 순간 사이에서 그들의 몸짓은 짙은 대비 속에 우아하게 자리한다. 멀리 담쟁이덩굴이 짙은 초록으로 숨을 쉬고, 도로 위의 시간은 잠시 멈춘 듯 고요하다. 금속의 차가운 감촉 속에 깃든 따스함, 아무 말 없이 서로를 바라보는 새들의 눈빛. 도심 속 흐름 속에서 조용히 존재감을 드러내는 이 새들은 잠시 멈춰 서서, 도시의 거친 속도와 지나간 순간의 고요를 다시 한번 마주하게 한다.

2-chōme-59 Nihonbashihamachō, Chuo City, Tokyo 103-0007

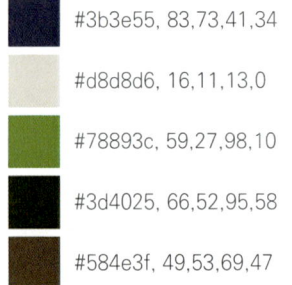

#3b3e55, 83,73,41,34

#d8d8d6, 16,11,13,0

#78893c, 59,27,98,10

#3d4025, 66,52,95,58

#584e3f, 49,53,69,47

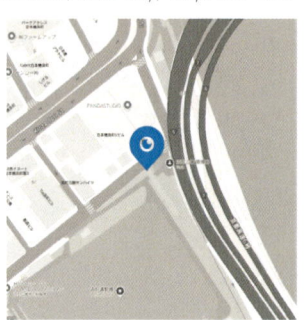

Beneath the massive overpass, the city breathes in a quiet yet unceasing rhythm. Cars slip through the concrete maze like fleeting shadows, each line connecting a fragment of urban life. Towering structures cast their shadows over the road above. In the brief light that seeps between steel pillars, a tranquil pause drifts through the heart of the city.

거대한 고가도로 아래, 도시는 고요하면서도 끊임없는 리듬 속에서 숨쉰다. 차들은 마치 스치는 그림자처럼 콘크리트 미로를 가로지르며, 각 선은 도시 삶의 한 조각을 이어간다. 그 위에 우뚝 서 있는 거대한 구조물은 도로 위로 그림자를 드리운다. 강철 기둥 사이로 스미는 잠시의 빛 속에서, 도심 속 고요한 멈춤이 흐른다.

MGJ6+JV9 Osaka, Japan

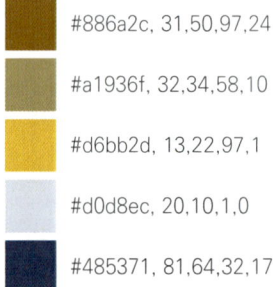

#886a2c, 31,50,97,24

#a1936f, 32,34,58,10

#d6bb2d, 13,22,97,1

#d0d8ec, 20,10,1,0

#485371, 81,64,32,17

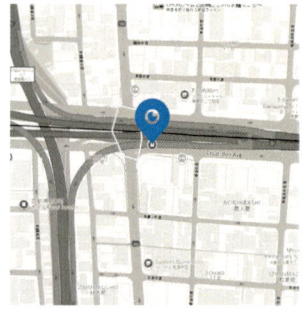

Morning begins at the railway crossing, where crimson trains awaken the day. As the locomotive glides slowly across tangled webs of electric wires, a lone cyclist pauses, leaving a gentle comma in the stream of daily life. Weathered traffic lights, timeworn buildings, and the humble things held in hand quietly radiate the warmth of a tranquil city. Along the tracks, traces of life linger—time softly intertwines in the contrast between the swift train and the languid bicycle. In this fleeting moment, the tender spirit of a small town quietly unfurls, and the breeze, ever faithful, carries with it stories yet untold.

아침은 붉은 전철이 시작되는 철도 건널목으로부터 시작된다. 기차가 전깃줄이 복잡하게 얽혀있는 선로를 천천히 가로지르면, 자전거를 탄 이가 잠시 멈춰 서서 일상의 흐름에 쉼표를 남긴다. 오래된 신호등과 낮은 건물, 그리고 손에 들려있는 소박함이 조용한 도시의 온기를 전한다. 철로를 따라 이어지는 삶의 흔적, 빠르게 지나가는 열차와 느릿한 자전거의 대비 속에서 시간은 부드럽게 교차한다. 잠시 머문 이 순간, 나라의 소도시 감성이 잔잔하게 번지고, 바람은 오늘도 새로운 이야기를 실어 온다.

MQWH+6R3 Nara, Japan

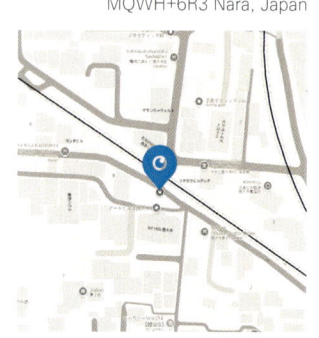

#84aacf, 58,19,7,0

#e3b92a, 5,27,96,0

#b78b2f, 18,45,96,6

#f1e4d3, 4,10,16,0

#9d3225, 18,94,97,10

The afternoon sunlight gently seeps through the letters of Shin-Omiya Station, weaving softness into the day. Overhead, electric wires stretch in parallel across the sky, threading the city's breath like silken strands, while traces of time settle quietly on rusted pillars and the red-brick walls. A cyclist's shadow glides across the crosswalk, and beside the crimson signal, a small moment of waiting pauses the rhythm of daily life. The hush of afternoon is filled with the quiet rituals of people's days. Sunbeams spill across the tracks, and between tangled wires, fragments of life drift by in silent procession.

오후의 햇살은 신오미야 역의 그림자를 비집고 부드럽게 스며든다. 전깃줄은 하늘에서 평행으로 달려 도시의 숨결을 실처럼 엮고, 오래된 시간의 흔적은 녹슨 기둥과 붉은 벽돌 담장 위에 사르르 내려앉는다. 횡단보도 위로 자전거를 타고 건너는 이의 그림자. 빨간 신호등 곁으로 작은 기다림이 일상의 흐름을 잠시 멈춘다. 오후의 정적을 채우는 사람들의 일상. 선로 위로 퍼지는 햇살과 복잡하게 얽힌 전선들 사이로 오가는 삶의 조각들이 조용히 흘러간다.

MRP6+2QP Nara, Japan

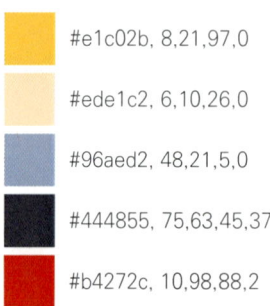

#e1c02b, 8,21,97,0

#ede1c2, 6,10,26,0

#96aed2, 48,21,5,0

#444855, 75,63,45,37

#b4272c, 10,98,88,2

In a quiet corner of Kyoto, tranquil time flows beneath the traditional shimenawa. Crimson, white, and blue ribbons sway gently in the morning breeze, softly whispering of centuries-old rituals of purification. The wooden gate, bearing the traces of ages, still stands within the current of history. Here, past and present intertwine, sacred and worldly realms divided by an invisible boundary. The living and the dead are embraced together. Every existing moment approaches like a prayer, each step embedded with the essence of tradition. All evil spirits are driven away, and every hope is quietly held within.

교토의 한적한 공간, 전통적인 시메나와 아래에서 고요한 시간이 흐른다. 붉고, 희고, 푸른 리본이 아침 바람에 살며시 흔들리며, 수 세기 동안 이어진 정화의 의식들을 조용히 속삭인다. 나무 문은 세월의 흔적을 간직한 채, 역사 속 흐름 속에서 여전히 거기 서 있다. 과거와 현재가 얽히는, 속세와 성스러움을 결계하는. 살아있는 자와 죽은 자를 아우르는. 존재하는 모든 순간이 기도처럼 다가오고, 한 걸음 한 걸음이 전통의 정수로 박혀있다. 모든 악귀를 쫓아내고, 모든 소망을 담은 채.

2Q2H+VC2 Kyoto, Japan

#b64a4c, 12,83,65,2

#d4c18c, 15,21,50,1

#553825, 37,71,85,56

#9f5e33, 22,69,89,12

#87462b, 25,79,91,23

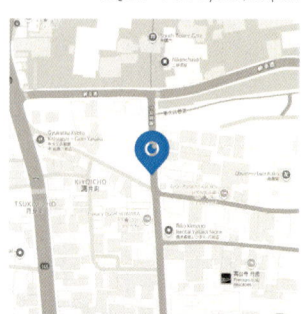

The gentle light of an autumn afternoon. The sky stretches wide, wishing to leave the day's warmth lingering in the breeze. In the quietude of Tennoji Zoo, where families wander, time seems to pause within the embrace of the trees. Children's laughter echoes from afar, carried on the wind like a fleeting melody. Sun-drenched scenes are painted into memory, as if watercolor reflections of the moment. A tranquil, unspoken connection with the world. The endless sky cradles the whispers of stories gone by, gazing down upon the serenity of everyday life.

가을 오후의 부드러운 빛. 하늘은 넓게 펼쳐져 하루의 따스함을 바람 속에 남기려 한다. 가족들이 산책하는 덴노지 동물원의 고요. 나무들의 품 안에서 시간이 잠시 멈춘 듯하다. 아이들의 웃음소리는 멀리서 울려 퍼지며, 바람에 실려와 순간의 멜로디처럼 들린다. 햇살에 한껏 물든 이 장면들은 순간을 반영한 수채화의 기억으로 남는다. 세상과의 평화로운 무언의 연결. 끝없이 펼쳐진 하늘은 지나간 이야기들의 속삭임을 품고, 평온한 일상을 내려다본다.

JGW7+Q56 Osaka, Japan

#adcbe8, 39,7,3,0

#4c92c6, 81,23,6,0

#cec636, 22,12,96,0

#baa036, 22,31,94,5

#b5702d, 16,62,96,5

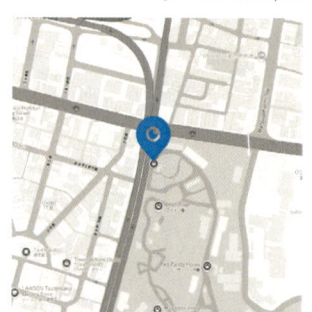

Sakuramon, the gateway leading to Osaka Castle, stands in silent endurance, bearing the weight of countless footsteps through the ages. The moat, now shrouded in a hush of green vines, invites me to imagine those long-ago days when peace was but a distant wish. I see crimson waves of blood filling the moat, the scars of war drifting on the wind, haunting and vivid. Now, vibrant green life veils the old pain, yet the cruel despair and memories of bloodshed may still breathe quietly beneath the surface of passing time.

오사카성으로 향하는 관문, 사쿠라마몬. 그 문은 셀 수 없는 발걸음의 무게를 조용히 견디며, 오랜 세월 침묵 속에 서 있다. 해자는 적막하도록 푸른 넝쿨에 감싸여 있지만, 나는 평화롭지 못했던 그 옛날의 수많은 날들을 마음속에 그려본다. 피로 물든 붉은 물결이 해자를 가득 채우고, 전쟁의 상흔이 바람결에 스며들던 순간들이 아릿하게 떠오른다. 지금은 생명의 초록이 옛 고통을 덮고 있으나, 죽음이 가득했던 잔인한 절망과 피의 기억은 여전히 세월의 수면 아래서 조용히 숨 쉬고 있을지도 모른다.

MGMF+XR7 Osaka, Japan

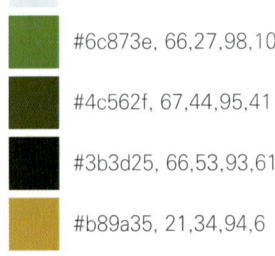

#d8dfef, 17,8,2,0

#6c873e, 66,27,98,10

#4c562f, 67,44,95,41

#3b3d25, 66,53,93,61

#b89a35, 21,34,94,6

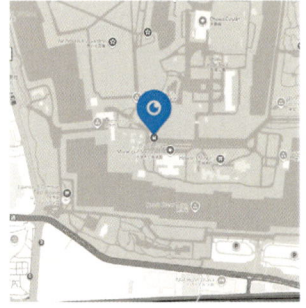

Beneath the blue sky, the city's light spills and spreads. Power lines weave overhead like tangled webs, while sunlight quietly slips between grey buildings. A four-leaf clover sign floats above the street, a small token of luck, as a cyclist crosses the road with gentle indifference. Glancing in opposite directions, pass each other-a fleeting intersection of the day's beginning and end. Trucks, cars, and small shadows fill the asphalt, while a distant breeze softly wraps the city's noise. In an ordinary alley where light and shadow mingle. The quiet rhythm of Osaka life flows toward Hommachi Station.

푸른 하늘 아래 도시의 빛이 번진다. 전깃줄이 거미줄처럼 얽혀 흐르고, 회색 건물 사이로 햇살이 조용히 스며든다. 네잎클로버 간판이 작은 행운처럼 거리에 떠 있고, 자전거를 탄 이가 무심히 길을 가로지른다. 서로 다른 방향을 바라보며 교차하는 순간, 바쁜 하루의 시작과 끝이 겹쳐진다. 트럭과 자동차, 그리고 작은 그림자들이 도로 위를 채우고, 멀리서 불어오는 바람이 도시의 소음을 부드럽게 감싼다. 평범한 골목에 스며든 빛과 그림자. 혼마치 역으로 향하는 오사카의 일상이 조용히 흐른다.

MGJ5+6VV Osaka, Japan

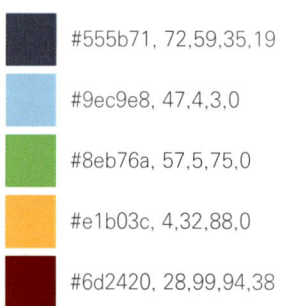

#555b71, 72,59,35,19
#9ec9e8, 47,4,3,0
#8eb76a, 57,5,75,0
#e1b03c, 4,32,88,0
#6d2420, 28,99,94,38

Time drifts slowly at Suzakumon, the ancient gate of Heijo Palace. The sun whispers an old hymn to its tranquil silhouette, holding time in a gentle suspension, letting it mellow and deepen. In late autumn, the soft rustle of feathery reeds brushing against the wind awakens a quietude, inviting it to rise. Old stories. Memories layered upon memories. Time upon time. All the meanings, gathered and folded, resting in the weight of ages.

시간이 느리게 천천히 흘러가는 헤이조궁의 관문인 수자쿠몬. 태양은 고요한 실루엣을 향해 오래된 찬가를 속삭인다. 시간을 느리게 잡아놓고 삭히는 풍경. 늦가을, 바람에 몸을 맡겨 제 몸을 부벼대는 깃털 같은 갈대의 사각거림이 고즈넉함을 소환해 기꺼이 깨워낸다. 오래된 이야기. 오래된 기억. 오래된 시간. 오래되어 겹겹히 쌓여 있는 함축들.

MQPV+WWM Nara, Japan

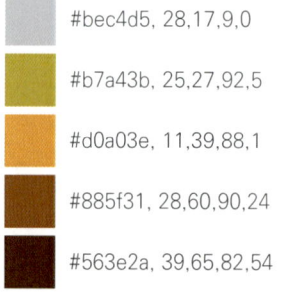

#bec4d5, 28,17,9,0

#b7a43b, 25,27,92,5

#d0a03e, 11,39,88,1

#885f31, 28,60,90,24

#563e2a, 39,65,82,54

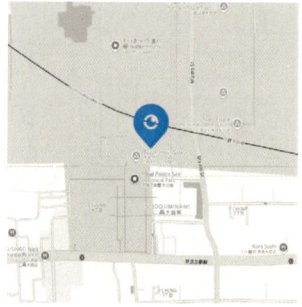

The sky of Osaka is divided by buildings and billboards, a patchwork above the city. The pedestrian overpass sways gently to the rhythm of urban life. Watchful billboards gaze down, their seductive eyes following those who pass beneath. In the city's heartbeat, pedestrians flow like fleeting shadows, slipping through the pulse of downtown. Quiet noise ripples between the gaps, echoing distantly, swallowed by the sharp lines of concrete towers. Here, time melts away, and those who pass are entwined in concrete, light, and ephemeral moments as they walk on.

건물과 광고판으로 구획된 오사카의 하늘. 보행자의 하늘 다리는 도시의 리듬에 맞춰 흔들린다. 관음하는 광고판. 유혹의 시선 아래로 지나가는 사람들. 도심의 맥박 속에서 스쳐 지나가는 그림자처럼 보행자들은 흐른다. 간격 사이에서 파동하는 조용한 소음은 멀리서 울리는 메아리처럼, 날카로운 건물들의 구획 속에 삼켜진다. 이 공간에서 시간은 녹아들고, 지나가는 이들은 콘크리트와 빛, 그리고 순간들 속에 얽힌채, 걷고 있다.

1 Chome Abenosuji, Abeno Ward, Osaka, 545-0052, Japan

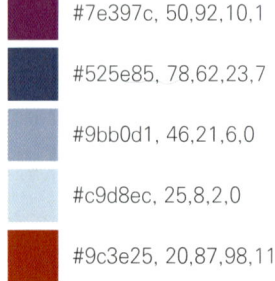

#7e397c, 50,92,10,1

#525e85, 78,62,23,7

#9bb0d1, 46,21,6,0

#c9d8ec, 25,8,2,0

#9c3e25, 20,87,98,11

A blush of pink breath seeps into the heart, and a quiet tremor gently soaks the soul. In tranquil gazes, ancient longing softly unfurls. The tender grain of countless moments brushes against my fingertips—a warmth that slowly radiates, old memories quietly blooming anew. Small wishes and delicate flutterings linger at the alley's end, carried by the breeze before fading away. Layers of time settle gently, leaving behind only silent peace. Subtle tremors linger in my gaze, and rosy afterglow spreads across the close of day. In this moment that flows as if stilled, a gentle anticipation remains, quietly nestled in a corner of my heart.

분홍빛 숨결이 마음에 스며들고, 조용한 떨림이 가슴을 적신다. 고요한 시선 속엔 오래된 그리움이 번지고. 여러 장면의 부드러운 결이 손끝을 스친다. 느리게 퍼지는 온기. 조용히 피어나는 오래된 기억. 작은 소망과 가벼운 설렘이 바람에 실려 골목 끝에 머물다 사라진다. 시간의 레이어가 천천히 내려앉고, 그곳엔 말없는 평화만 남는다. 작은 떨림은 시선에 머물고, 분홍빛 여운이 하루의 끝에 번진다. 멈춘 듯 흐르는 순간, 마음 한켠에 잔잔한 기대감이 남는다.

XQXH+9JJ Kyoto, Japan

#3f5b9a, 89,64,7,0

#45659d, 86,57,11,1

#75a0cd, 64,23,5,0

#3e342b, 53,63,71,67

#b5622f, 14,71,93,4

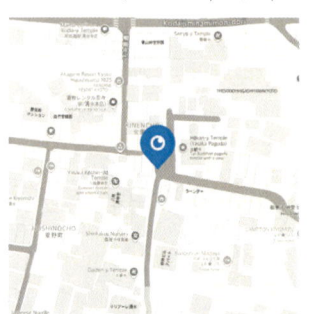

The breath of a street on Osaka's Chuo-dori drifts quietly beneath the concrete. Hidden pathways beneath the earth are unveiled in strokes of white paint. The temporarily patched asphalt is gentle yet resolute, holding the silent whispers of pipes below. The painted lines are fleeting, yet they cradle both what once was and what is yet to come. Traces etched upon the road will soon fade from memory, but my frame remembers. In these brief marks of paint, the city is quietly being reborn.

오사카 주오도리 어느 거리의 숨결은 콘크리트 아래로 고요히 흐른다. 하얀색 페인트로 노출시킨 땅 속의 보이지 않는 경로들. 임시로 덮인 아스팔트는 부드럽지만 단단히 땅 속 파이프들의 조용한 속삭임을 품고 있다. 그려진 선은 일시적이지만, 무엇이었고 무엇이 될지를 품고 있다. 거리 위에 새겨진 흔적은 곧 잊혀지겠지만, 나의 크롭은 기억한다. 잠깐의 페인트 흔적 속에서, 도시는 조용히 다시 태어나고 있음을.

2 Chome Tokiwamachi, Chuo Ward, Osaka, 540-0028, Japan

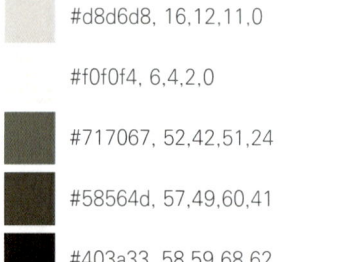

#d8d6d8, 16,12,11,0

#f0f0f4, 6,4,2,0

#717067, 52,42,51,24

#58564d, 57,49,60,41

#403a33, 58,59,68,62

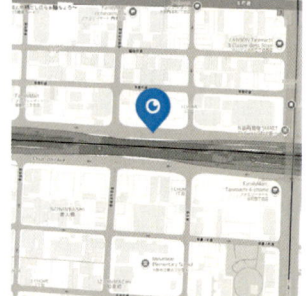

The slow-spreading warmth of Saidaiji, an ancient temple over a thousand years old. A gentle peace settles quietly within the heart. Serene breaths envelop tranquility, as lingering longing softly descends. When the grain of light brushes my fingertips, old memories gently sway. Time flows as if stilled, and silent gazes linger without a word. Even a single breath of wind stirs the heart, a delicate tremor spreading like a sigh. With every deep exhale, a slow relief unfurls. In the moment when everything gently sinks, quiet peace soaks into the soul.

천년이 넘은 고찰, 사이다이지의 느리게 번지는 온기. 마음 속에 내려앉는 잔잔한 평화. 고요한 숨결이 평정을 감싸고, 남겨진 그리움이 조용히 내려앉는다. 빛의 결이 손끝을 어루만지면, 오래된 기억이 부드럽게 흔들린다. 멈춘 듯 흐르는 시간, 아무 말 없이 머무는 시선. 바람 한 줄기에도 마음이 흔들리고, 가벼운 떨림이 숨결처럼 번진다. 깊은 숨을 내쉴 때마다 퍼지는 느린 안도. 모든 것이 천천히 가라앉는 순간, 고요한 평화가 마음을 적신다.

1-chōme-1 Saidaiji Shibachō, Nara, 631-0825, Japan

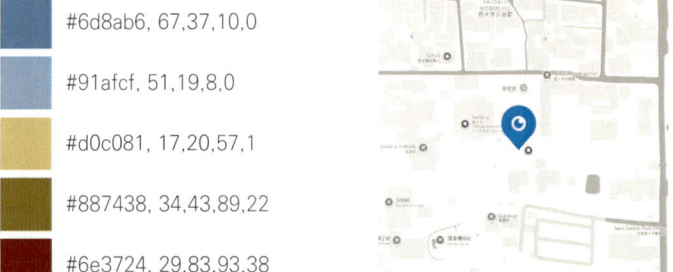

#6d8ab6, 67,37,10,0

#91afcf, 51,19,8,0

#d0c081, 17,20,57,1

#887438, 34,43,89,22

#6e3724, 29,83,93,38

The quiet resonance of life weaves and flows through the streets. The air of the seasons carries delicate echoes with every step. People, adorned in the hues of the season, ascend the hills. Along the road, Kyoto's old-fashioned shops line up gracefully, whispering tales where the past brushes against the present. Amid the bustling crowds, the street breathes slowly. Tradition and modernity intertwine, alive in their shared rhythm. Distant mountains, sitting quietly apart, watch over it all, remembering each scene as it drifts through time.

삶의 고요한 울림이 거리를 통해 얽히며 흐른다. 계절의 공기는 발걸음마다 섬세한 메아리를 싣는다. 계절의 색을 입고 언덕을 오르는 사람들. 고풍스러운 교토의 낮은 상점들이 길을 따라 늘어서, 현재와 맞닿은 과거의 이야기까지를 한꺼번에 속삭인다. 혼잡한 인파 속에서, 거리는 느리게 숨을 쉰다. 전통과 현대가 리듬 속에서 얽힌 채 살아있고. 멀치감치 비켜 앉아있는 산은 그 모든 것을 조용히 지켜보며 시간 속 장면을 기억한다.

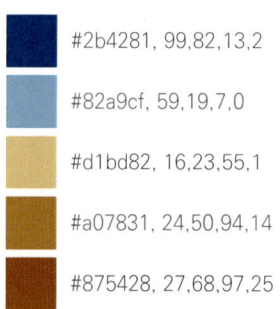

#2b4281, 99,82,13,2
#82a9cf, 59,19,7,0
#d1bd82, 16,23,55,1
#a07831, 24,50,94,14
#875428, 27,68,97,25

XQWM+248 Kyoto, Japan

The tangled pulse of the city thrums restlessly. Abeno Bridge silently witnesses the passage of time. Swift, unyielding trains cut through the scene like fleeting thoughts, while the everyday lives of passersby cast brief shadows as they walk without a glance. The gentle afternoon light momentarily preserves the world within the ceaselessly moving city, and each short step leaves a comma-like trace—a fleeting pause—amid the flowing landscape.

얼기설기 얽힌 도시의 맥박 소리. 아베노 다리는 시간의 흐름을 묵묵히 지켜본다. 빠르고 거침없는 열차는 지나가는 생각처럼 이 장면을 가로지르고, 그 위를 무심히 걷는 사람들의 일상에는 짧은 그림자가 스쳐 지나간다. 오후의 부드러운 빛은 끝없이 움직이는 도시 속에서 세상을 잠시 박제시키고, 짧은 발걸음 하나하나는 흐르는 풍경 속에서 쉼표같은 찰나의 자국을 남긴다.

JGW7+Q56 Osaka, Japan

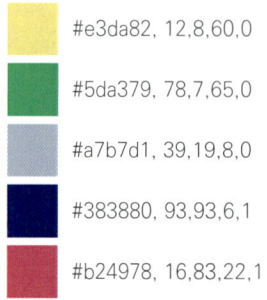

#e3da82, 12,8,60,0

#5da379, 78,7,65,0

#a7b7d1, 39,19,8,0

#383880, 93,93,6,1

#b24978, 16,83,22,1

Within the quiet embrace of Okamoto Orimono shop, time flows like fabric draped upon the walls, and threads woven long ago entwine the stories of passing years. In the photograph, memories smile softly in silence, as if they are a delicate fragment woven into Kyoto's history. Here, between the folds of kimono textiles and the warm glow of stained glass, memories linger—like the whispers of a forgotten era, like a fleeting vision resting in the gaze.

오카모토 오리모노 상점의 고요한 품 안에서, 시간은 벽에 걸린 직물처럼 흐르고, 오래 전 직조된 실은 지난 세월의 이야기를 엮어내고 있다. 사진 속에서 기억들이 조용히 미소짓고 있다. 교토의 역사 속에서 섬세하게 짜여진 한 조각인 듯. 여기, 기모노 직물의 주름과 따스한 스테인드글라스의 빛 사이에서 추억은 맴돌고 있다. 잊힌 시대의 속삭임처럼. 눈동자에 머무는 환상처럼.

Higashiyama Ward, Kiyomizu, Kyoto, 605-0862, Japan

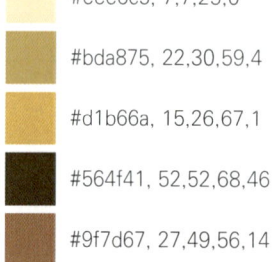

#eee6c5, 7,7,25,0

#bda875, 22,30,59,4

#d1b66a, 15,26,67,1

#564f41, 52,52,68,46

#9f7d67, 27,49,56,14

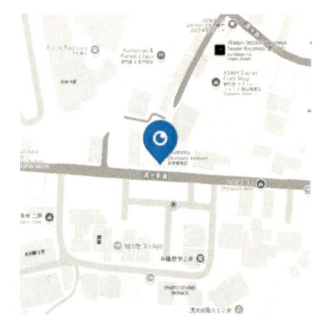

A long, ascending path leads to Kiyomizudera Temple. The hems of two women's kimonos flutter softly. Their footsteps flow gently along the road, their figures woven together like fine threads and bathed in the afternoon sunlight. A faint fragrance drifts from the sleeves as the breeze passes by. Their shadows, walking side by side, stretch long across the ground. The wooden frames of old shop doors, whispers seeping beneath paper lanterns, and the grain of time accumulating in every alleyway. A sigh as light as breath seeps into each careful step. In this tranquil anticipation, the silhouettes of the two women slowly unfurl along the curves of season and memory.

기요즈미데라 사원으로 이어지는 긴 오르막길. 두 여인의 기모노 자락이 살랑인다. 발걸음이 조심스레 길을 따라 흐르고, 고운 색실처럼 엮인 뒷모습이 오후 햇살에 물든다. 바람이 스치는 소매 끝에서 번지는 옅은 향기. 나란히 걷는 그림자가 길게 늘어진다. 오래된 상점의 목재 문틀. 종이 등불 아래 스며드는 속삭임. 골목마다 쌓여가는 시간의 결. 숨결처럼 가벼운 한숨이 천천히 오르는 발끝으로 스며든다. 고요한 설렘 속, 두 여인의 실루엣이 계절과 기억의 곡선을 따라 천천히 번진다.

Japan, 605-0862 Kyoto, Higashiyama Ward, Kiyomizu, 1-chōme

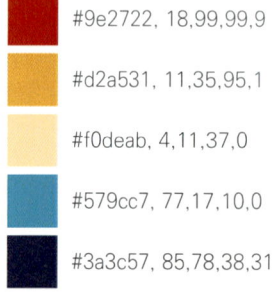

#9e2722, 18,99,99,9

#d2a531, 11,35,95,1

#f0deab, 4,11,37,0

#579cc7, 77,17,10,0

#3a3c57, 85,78,38,31

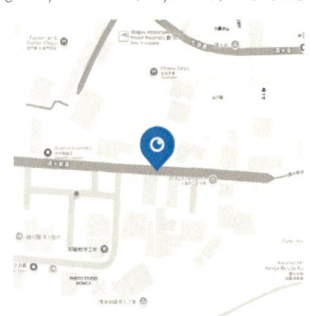

In the heart of the city, at Tennoji Zoo, lions bask in the gentle afternoon sunlight, sprawled in quiet repose. Their golden fur is kissed by the warmth of time. Behind them, the sharp glass tower of Abeno Harukas slices the sky, a stark contrast to human ambition. The concrete jungle, alive with the pulse of those who dwell in the present, seems to whisper tales of forgotten times beneath the canopy of green. In the hush of the zoo, nature and architecture watch over each other, dancing a silent ballet.

도심 속, 덴노지 동물원. 사자들은 조용한 오후 햇살을 듬뿍 받으며 드러누워 있다. 황금빛 털은 시간의 온기로 입맞춤을 받는다. 그들 뒤로 아베노하루카스의 날카로운 유리 타워가 인간의 야망을 대조하며 쪼개낸다. 녹음 속의 잊혀진 시간의 이야기가 속삭여지는 것만 같은 콘크리트 정글은 현재를 살아가는 사람들의 맥박을 품고 있다. 동물원의 고요 속에서 자연과 건축은 말 없는 춤을 추며 서로를 지켜본다.

MG35+67W Osaka, Japan

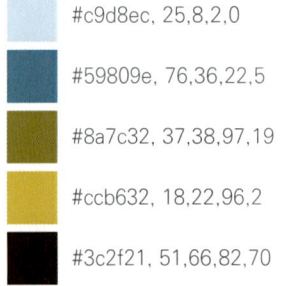

#c9d8ec, 25,8,2,0
#59809e, 76,36,22,5
#8a7c32, 37,38,97,19
#ccb632, 18,22,96,2
#3c2f21, 51,66,82,70

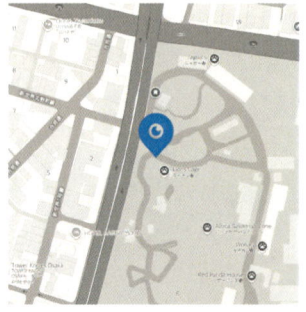

In the tranquil temple grounds bathed in sunset, the tiled roof of an old sanctuary bears the sky between ancient trees. Footsteps quietly sink into the worn stone path, and a deer approaches, dissolving the boundary between the everyday and the extraordinary. Warm light embraces crimson maple leaves, and in the still air, gazes meet and time seems to pause. The shadow of a venerable tree, wooden pillars of the temple, and the gentle murmur of voices spreading in the evening dusk. Here, the close of day seeps in slowly, leaving a quiet sense of wonder in this landscape where nature and people are gently intertwined.

석양이 내려앉은 고즈넉한 경내, 나무와 고목 사이로 오래된 사찰의 기와지붕이 묵직하게 하늘을 받치고 있다. 오래된 돌바닥 위로 사람들의 발걸음이 조용히 스며들고, 사슴 한 마리가 다가와 일상과 비일상의 경계를 허문다. 따스한 빛이 붉은 단풍을 감싸고, 고요한 공기 속에서 서로를 바라보는 시선들이 잠시 시간을 멈춘다. 늙은 고목의 그림자. 사찰의 나무 기둥. 저녁의 어스름 속에 번지는 사람들의 낮은 목소리. 이곳에서는 하루의 끝이 천천히 스며들며, 자연과 사람이 어우러진 풍경이 조용한 감동으로 남는다.

MRMQ+VXF Nara, Japan

#cbd6eb, 23,10,2,0

#eccc02, 8,18,99,0

#3e372b, 56,60,75,66

#ca8b23, 13,50,99,3

#b06526, 19,68,98,8

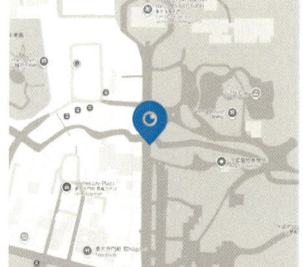

On a tranquil afternoon, Narrow, winding alleys in Nara unfold like a whispered poem between rooftops crowned with traditional tiles. On the sunlit gray pavement, elongated shadows trace the rhythm of solitude, while tangled wires atop utility poles speak of countless streams of time crossing the blue sky. In a corner mirror, the solitary step of a passerby is reflected-quietly awakening the slow, living breath of this village, woven into the stillness of its humble lanes.

고요한 낮, 나라의 좁고 구불구불한 골목은 전통 기와가 얹어진 지붕 사이로 속삭이듯 펼쳐진 한 편의 시이다. 햇살 머문 회색 포장 도로 위에는 길게 드리운 그림자가 고독의 리듬을 그리며, 머리 위 전신주의 복잡한 전선들은 푸른 하늘을 가로지르는 무수한 시간의 흐름을 이야기한다. 구석진 반사경 속에 비친 한 사람의 외로운 걸음이, 소박한 골목길의 정적 속에 묵묵히 살아 숨 쉬는 이 마을의 느린 호흡을 일깨운다.

MQVH+HCR Nara, Japan

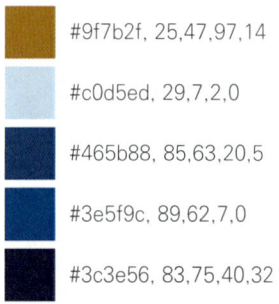

#9f7b2f, 25,47,97,14

#c0d5ed, 29,7,2,0

#465b88, 85,63,20,5

#3e5f9c, 89,62,7,0

#3c3e56, 83,75,40,32

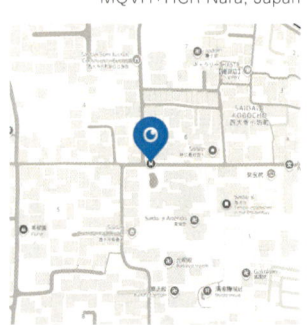

A tranquil temple. Through the eaves, whispers of time drift softly. Wooden prayer plaques, carrying people's wishes, sway in the breeze, clicking gently in their silent prayers. Warm, gentle autumn sunlight pours into Kyoto's Hokoji Temple-a place where tradition and the present moment meet, where past and present flow as one. The spirit of faith lingers like a subtle fragrance, and hopes spread quietly, carried on the murmurs of the wind.

고요한 사원. 처마의 사잇길로 시간의 속삭임이 떠돈다. 사람들의 소망이 담긴 나무 기도판이 바람에 실려 딸깍딸각 소리를 내면서 흔들리며 기도 중이다. 교토의 호코지 사원 속으로 따뜻하고 온화한 가을 햇살이 쏟아진다. 전통과 순간이 만나는 곳. 과거와 현재가 한 줄기로 흐르는 곳. 믿음의 정신은 향기처럼 남겨지고, 소망은 바람의 속삭임을 타고 은은하게 퍼져나간다.

527-2 Chayacho, Higashiyama Ward, Kyoto, 605-0931, Japan

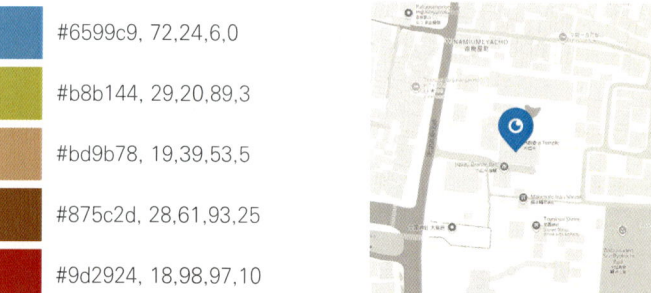

#6599c9, 72,24,6,0

#b8b144, 29,20,89,3

#bd9b78, 19,39,53,5

#875c2d, 28,61,93,25

#9d2924, 18,98,97,10

Into the arteries of sturdy railway tracks, the underpass draws a quiet breath. A cyclist, hood pulled tight, glides into a lake-like shade woven by the dazzling midday light and gentle shadows, each pedal stroke releasing whispered prayers. Cars do not hurry, spilling white silence slowly onto the road, their engines murmuring the street's languid pulse. The traveler hums the song of rusted steel beams and tangled wires, as if memory itself is fused with iron and concrete. Here, "movement" becomes a ritual of contemplation-two beings, one of speed and one of stillness, drifting together in the weightlessness of time.

굵직한 철길의 동맥 속으로 지하도는 고요한 숨을 들이쉰다. 후드를 단단히 여민 자전거 타는 사람은 한낮의 눈부신 빛과 부드러운 그림자가 엮어낸 호수 같은 그늘 속으로 미끄러지듯 나아가며, 발걸음마다 속삭임 같은 기도를 풀어놓는다. 자동차들은 서두르지 않고, 천천히 흰 고요를 길 위에 흘리며, 엔진의 낮은 귓속말로 거리의 느린 맥박을 훑는다. 여행자는 녹슨 철골과 뒤엉킨 전선의 노래를 흥얼이며, 마치 기억이 강철과 콘크리트에 혼합된 듯한 풍경을 만든다. 이곳에서 '이동'은 숙고의 의식. 속도와 정적이 어우러진 두 존재가, 시간의 무중력 속에서 함께 가만히 흐른다.

MQRM+WX7 Nara, Japan

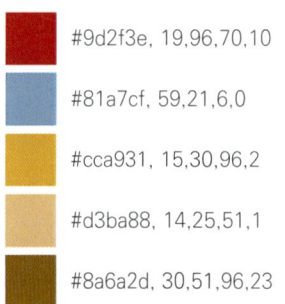

#9d2f3e, 19,96,70,10

#81a7cf, 59,21,6,0

#cca931, 15,30,96,2

#d3ba88, 14,25,51,1

#8a6a2d, 30,51,96,23

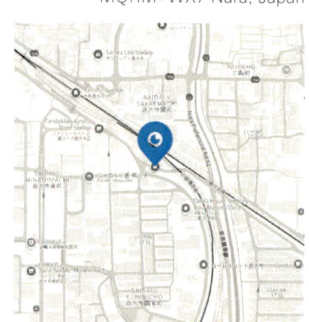

Inside the small station, evening sunlight stretches long across the platform floor. People with weary shoulders quietly pass through the ticket gates. Destinations flicker on the departure board. The weight of the day lingers at the fingertips holding their bags. As the sound of the departing train fades, footsteps scatter toward different homes. Someone pauses on a bench to catch their breath. Glances meet briefly in the glow of a phone screen. Warmth lingers in the narrow corridor. In the corners of the station, small stories gather, each dissolving into the evening air at its own gentle pace.

작은 역사 안, 저녁 햇살이 플랫폼 바닥에 길게 스며든다. 피곤한 어깨를 늘어뜨린 사람들이 조용히 개찰구를 지난다. 전광판에 깜빡이는 행선지. 가방을 든 손끝에 하루의 무게가 묻어난다. 기차가 멀어지는 소리와 함께, 서로 다른 집을 향해 흩어지는 발걸음. 벤치에 앉아 잠시 숨을 고르는 이. 휴대폰 불빛 아래 스치는 눈빛. 좁은 통로에 남겨진 따뜻한 온기. 역 구석에 쌓인 작은 이야기들이 저마다의 속도로 저녁 공기 속에 녹아든다.

MRP6+5FQ Nara, Japan

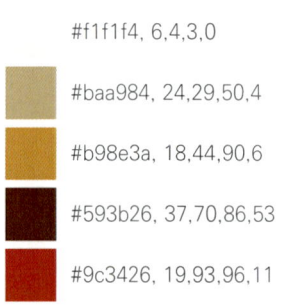
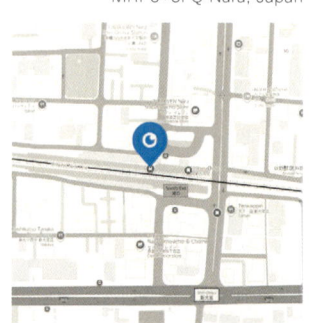

#f1f1f4, 6,4,3,0

#baa984, 24,29,50,4

#b98e3a, 18,44,90,6

#593b26, 37,70,86,53

#9c3426, 19,93,96,11

Between soaring glass towers, golden ginkgo leaves blaze like flames, while warm footsteps etch the city's frozen streets. Where cold steel meets the breath of ancient trees, the season stands at that fragile edge, quietly smiling. Winter sunlight softly settles on the white pavement, and sky's reflection on towering buildings illuminates the day with gentle light. Amidst the city's relentless rush, life briefly slips, then regains its steady rhythm. In Marunouchi Park, beneath endless skyscrapers, centuries-old ginkgo leaves drift silently, and even amid modern clamor, nature's whisper hums softly. The ceaseless pulse of the world pauses for a moment, as the humble heartbeat of life awakens our souls anew.

고층 유리 건물 사이로 노란 은행잎이 불꽃처럼 물들고, 도심 속엔 따스한 발걸음이 새겨진다. 차가운 철골과 나무의 숨결이 만나는 곳, 계절은 그 경계에 서서 조용히 미소 짓는다. 하얀 바닥 위로 겨울 햇살이 내려앉고, 빌딩에 반사된 하늘빛은 오늘을 환하게 비춘다. 분주한 도시 한가운데, 삶은 잠시 미끄러지다 다시 중심을 잡는다. 마루노우치 공원, 끝없이 솟은 마천루 아래 수백 년 묵은 은행나무 잎사귀가 고요히 흩날리며, 현대의 소음 속에서도 자연의 숨결이 고요히 울린다. 바쁘게 돌아가는 세상의 리듬은 잠시 멈추고, 소박한 삶의 맥박이 우리의 마음을 깨운다.

MQJ8+G2R Chiyoda City, Tokyo, Japan

#d3b68c, 13,28,47,1

#d0aa30, 12,31,96,1

#475831, 73,41,98,38

#b6d1ea, 34,7,3,0

#475d85, 84,61,23,7

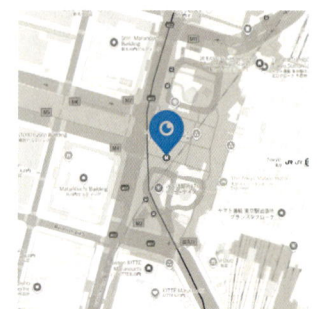

Amidst the radiant autumn, Kyoto softly whispers its unchanging tales. A couple in white kimonos preserves a fleeting moment, as if pausing time itself. Crimson leaves cradle the season's warmth, quietly stirring the heart and approaching like a reverent homage to history. On this street where past and present entwine, the legacy of culture breathes and memories waltz through time. Even their preserved memories seem to dance in the gentle air.

찬란한 가을 속에서, 교토는 그 변하지 않는 이야기를 속삭인다. 순간을 박제하는 하얀 기모노의 커플. 붉은 잎들이 계절의 따스함을 품고, 그 마음을 고요히 감동시키며 역사를 향한 경배처럼 다가온다. 과거와 현재가 얽히는 이 거리는 문화의 유산을 품고, 기억의 시간을 춤추듯 숨 쉰다. 박제된 그들의 기억도 춤춘다.

2Q2H+VC2 Kyoto, Japan

#b12727, 11,98,93,3

#3878b2, 90,39,6,0

#3e81b4, 87,33,10,0

#9da03d, 41,23,95,5

#724929, 31,69,91,37

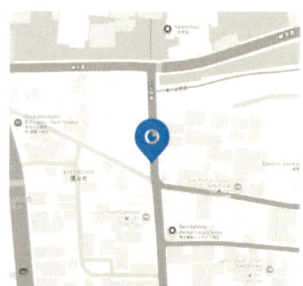

In the quiet embrace of Sotokanda, just beyond the dazzling noise and ceaseless flow of Akihabara, sunlight slips between tall buildings, catching the shimmer of yellow kindergarten hats. The season clings gently to the tips of leaves, and a banner sways in the breeze, whispering memories of passing time. A pointed spire converses with the sky, while green railings guard the children's path. Laughter and footsteps fill the alley, a fleeting glimpse of innocence nestled within the city's daily rhythm. On this tranquil afternoon, the time of childhood quietly drifts through the stillness.

아키하바라의 화려한 소음과 수많은 사람들의 흐름의 뒷 켠, 고요한 소토칸다. 빌딩 사이 햇살이 스며들고, 아이들의 노란 유치원 모자가 반짝거린다. 계절은 나뭇잎 끝에 걸려 있고, 현수막이 바람을 불러 계절을 기억하게 한다. 하늘과 대화를 나누는 뾰족한 첨탑, 아이들의 길을 지켜주는 초록 펜스. 골목을 채우는 웃음과 발걸음, 도시의 일상 속 가장 순수한 풍경이 지나간다. 조용한 오후, 고요한 이 거리엔 어린 시절의 시간이 흐르고 있다.

3-chōme-10-9 Sotokanda, Chiyoda City, Tokyo 101-0021

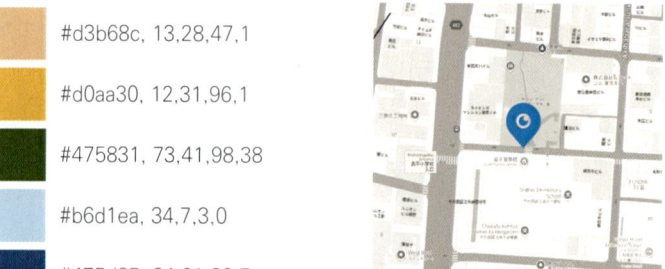

#d3b68c, 13,28,47,1

#d0aa30, 12,31,96,1

#475831, 73,41,98,38

#b6d1ea, 34,7,3,0

#475d85, 84,61,23,7

In a quiet corner of a narrow alley in Saidaiji Kobocho, a humble wooden box cradles emerald broccoli and silvery radishes side by side. An old cardboard sign leans against the wall, swaying softly in the breeze, guarding the alley like a silent verse. Gentle daylight wraps the box, and the freshness of vegetables fills the small space. The texture of weathered bricks and wood, along with the traces of caring hands, whispers of simple abundance. In the stillness of early afternoon, the little alley becomes a line of poetry woven into the heart of daily life. When the breeze passes by, the scent of vegetables and sunlight mingle, leaving a quiet warmth in the ordinariness of the day.

사이다이지 코보초의 좁은 골목 한켠, 소박한 나무 상자 안에 에메랄드 빛 브로콜리와 은빛 무가 나란히 놓여 있다. 낡은 골판지 표지판은 벽에 기대어, 바람에 흔들리며 조용한 시구처럼 골목을 지킨다. 부드러운 낮빛이 상자 위를 감싸고, 채소의 싱그러움이 작은 공간을 가득 채운다. 오래된 벽돌과 나무의 결, 그리고 손길이 닿은 자국이 소박한 풍요를 속삭인다. 이른 오후의 고요함 속에서, 작은 골목은 일상의 시 한 구절이 되어 마음에 스며든다. 바람이 지나가면, 채소의 향과 햇살이 어우러져, 평범한 하루에 잔잔한 온기를 남긴다.

MQWH+7J7 Nara, Japan

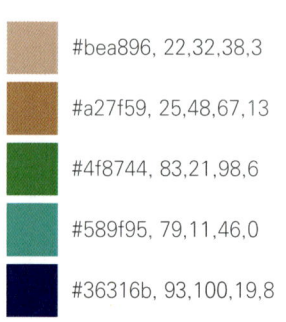

#bea896, 22,32,38,3

#a27f59, 25,48,67,13

#4f8744, 83,21,98,6

#589f95, 79,11,46,0

#36316b, 93,100,19,8

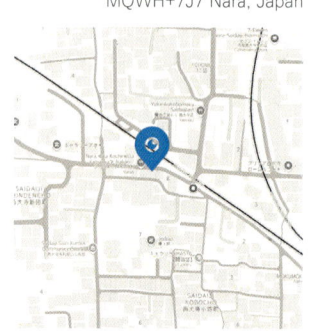

Like a forgotten memory, the Kamo River in Kyoto has long begun to whisper softly and low. The old, timeworn houses have quietly watched the passage of time for ages. The blue sky, distant as an unattainable dream, seems to shower only indifferent blessings upon the stories etched into the walls of these buildings. Power lines bridge past and present. As crimson autumn leaves add fleeting color to the stillness, in this tranquil moment, the city breathes slowly. In the breath suspended somewhere between the old and the new, Kyoto lingers quietly, poised between eras.

잊혀진 기억처럼 부드럽게 나지막히 속삭이기 시작한지 이미 오래된 교토의 카모 강. 또한 이미 오래 전부터 시간의 흐름을 조용히 지켜본 낡고 오래된 집들. 파란 하늘은 닿을 수 없는 꿈처럼 멀고, 건물의 벽에 새겨진 이야기에 무심한 축복만 쏟아붓는 듯하다. 과거와 현재를 이어주는 전선. 가을의 붉은 나뭇잎들이 그 고요함에 덧없이 색을 더하는 가운데, 이 고요한 순간, 도시는 천천히 숨을 쉬고 있다. 오래된 것과 새로운 것 그 사이 어딘가에 걸린 듯한 그 숨결 속에서.

XQR9+P2F Kyoto, Japan

#3b629b, 90,59,10,1
#a9cbe8, 41,6,3,0
#a08f3e, 31,34,89,11
#89753a, 34,43,88,22
#3b3829, 61,57,80,65

On a quiet evening, the cat mural gazes cautiously, as if secretly watching the passing strangers. Its eyes are wide and patient, following each fleeting moment, silently observing the flow of life within the alley. The city's pulse is felt softly in every footstep, yet the cat remains perfectly still. It savors the stories of those who pass by, while neon lights tint the night, painting the memories of this place in gentle, wistful hues.

조용한 저녁, 고양이 벽화는 마치 지나가는 행인을 훔쳐보듯 조심스럽게 응시한다. 그 눈은 크고 인내심 깊게, 빠르게 지나가는 순간을 하나하나 따라가며, 골목 속 삶의 흐름을 묵묵히 지켜본다. 도시의 맥박은 발걸음 속에서 부드럽게 느껴지지만, 고양이는 여전히 미동이 없다. 지나가는 이들의 이야기를 곱씹으며, 네온 불빛은 밤을 물들이며 그 곳의 기억들을 아련하게 그려낸다.

458-1 Higashiuoyachō, Nakagyo Ward, Kyoto, 604-8055, Japan

#e3b92a, 5,27,96,0

#715f2f, 39,50,92,34

#9f8f32, 32,33,98,11

#d4d3c5, 18,12,22,0

#2f5571, 94,56,35,18

A thousand years seep into wooden pillars, and mist settling over the mountain temple lingers like an ancient prayer. Footprints gather on each step, while the bell's chime drifts quietly along the valley. Crimson maples and emerald moss carry the breath of the seasons. Tourists in elegant kimonos move gently through the tranquil grounds, capturing memories as they go. The sound of flowing water becomes the backdrop to old tales. Beneath tiled roofs, wishes are layered one upon another. The scent of incense drifts on the breeze, wrapping the temple in fragrance. Countless meetings and farewells pass through this place. Under moonlight, the silent night deepens the texture of history-Kiyomizudera, a name steeped in the richness of time.

천년의 시간이 나무 기둥에 스며들고, 산사에 내리는 안개가 오래된 기도처럼 머문다. 계단마다 발자국이 쌓이고, 종소리는 계곡을 따라 조용히 퍼진다. 계절의 숨결을 전하는 붉은 단풍과 푸른 이끼. 기모노를 곱게 차려입은 관광객들이 고요한 경내를 천천히 오르내리며, 추억을 기록한다. 흐르는 물소리가 옛 이야기의 배경이 되는. 기와지붕 아래 차곡차곡 쌓이는 염원. 향 내음은 바람에 실려 경내를 감싸고. 수많은 인연과 이별이 이곳을 지나간다. 달빛 아래 고요한 밤이 역사의 결을 더하며, 기요미즈데라. 이름 속에는 세월의 깊이가 녹진하게 녹아있다.

XQWM+574 Kyoto, Japan

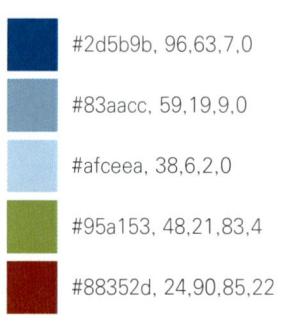

#2d5b9b, 96,63,7,0

#83aacc, 59,19,9,0

#afceea, 38,6,2,0

#95a153, 48,21,83,4

#88352d, 24,90,85,22

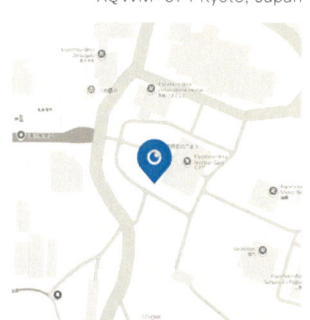

At the edge of Sarusawa-ike Pond, rosy twilight softly caresses the mirror-like surface of the water. The silhouette of traditional tiled roofs shimmers in gentle echoes across the calm ripples, and autumn's stillness, steeped in nostalgia, seeps into each leaf. When a breeze drifts by, crimson leaves slowly settle onto the water, and the tiny waves whisper ancient stories. Time holds its breath, and tranquil harmony lingers in the afterglow of night. Shadows along the pond stand quietly, holding the fading light until the very end. Sunset hues ripple across the water's scales, and the warmth of the vanishing day remains quietly in a corner of the heart.

사루사와 이케 연못 가장자리에서 불그레한 황혼이 거울처럼 맑은 수면을 부드럽게 어루만진다. 전통 기와집의 실루엣이 고요한 메아리처럼 잔잔한 물결 위에 일렁이고, 가을의 정적은 향수를 담아 잎사귀 하나하나에 스며든다. 바람 한 줄기가 스치면, 붉게 물든 잎이 물 위로 천천히 내려앉고, 잔물결은 오래된 이야기를 속삭인다. 시간은 숨을 고르고, 평온한 조화가 밤의 여운 속에 흐른다. 연못가에 선 그림자들은 고요히 늘어서서, 저물어가는 빛을 마지막까지 머금는다. 물비늘 위로 번지는 노을빛, 그리고 사라져가는 하루의 온기가 마음 한켠에 잔잔히 남는다.

MRJJ+M4W Nara, Japan

#6c7187, 63,50,29,10

#594a2f, 45,56,83,49

#c0b1a7, 23,28,29,2

#d28659, 6,56,68,0

#b55731, 13,77,90,3

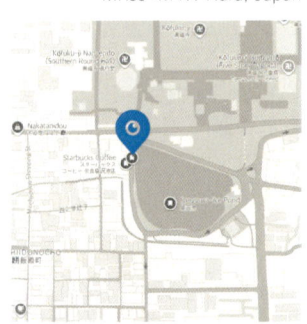

The bustling streets of Kyoto flow through time like gentle waves. Those dressed in kimono glide softly, like memories wrapped in silk, their footsteps carrying echoes of the past into the present. Within these ancient souls, the pulse of now beats quietly. When sunlight spills gold across the cobblestones, I recall distant moments—like the Beatles crossing Abbey Road. An homage in kimono, traversing the crosswalk of history and memory. Here, each fleeting instant is captured and cropped, drifting away in the shadows of tradition and progress.

교토의 분주한 거리는 부드러운 파도처럼 시간을 흘러보낸다. 기모노를 입은 사람들은 실크로 감싼 추억처럼 부드럽게 미끄러지며, 그들의 발걸음을 과거의 울림으로부터 현재로 옮겨낸다. 오래된 영혼 속에서 현재의 맥박을 뛴다. 햇살이 돌길 위로 황금빛을 쏟을 때, 나는 먼 순간을 떠올린다. 비틀즈가 애비로드를 건널 때처럼. 역사와 기억의 횡단보도를 건너는 기모노의 오마주. 이곳에서 순간은 잡혀 크롭되고, 전통과 진보의 그림자 속에서 떠나가고 있다.

Shijo-sagaru, Hanamikoji, Higashiyama-ku, Kyoto, 604-0075, Japan

Crimson leaves fall, like memories whispered to the earth. The ancient pagoda stands in stillness, silently watching over the heart of Kyoto. Beyond lies the land of the present. As if a boundary has been drawn, the temple and Kyoto Tower face each other in sharp, silent dialogue. The old and the new are quietly embraced, while the mountains look on, bearing witness to both. Time itself seems to pause in reverence for this moment.

붉은 잎들이 속삭이는 기억처럼 후두둑 떨어진다. 고요히 서 있는 고대의 탑은 교토의 도심을 침묵 속에서 지켜본다. 저 너머에는 현재의 땅. 경계가 쳐진 듯, 사원과 교토 타워는 뾰족하게 대결하며 서로를 바라본다. 옛 것과 새것은 조용히 품어지고, 산들은 둘 다의 상징을 묵묵히 지켜보는 가운데. 시간이란 것이 그 순간을 경배하듯 잠시 멈추어 서 있는 듯하다.

XQVM+XGP Kyoto, Japan

#586887, 74,54,26,9

#afbcd2, 36,18,9,0

#a1883b, 28,38,90,13

#6f3120, 28,88,96,37

#9c3225, 19,94,97,11

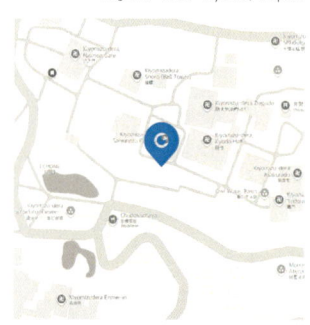

CROP in TOKYO, OSAKA

NIGHT

밤

A quiet night encountered on the streets of Chuo, Tokyo. Traffic lights whisper distant commands, exhaling gentle silence. The flickering glow of streetlamps seeps into the road. This path, once crossed by countless footsteps, now lies empty, drifting into slumber. Shadows stretch long into the night. The city's lights live on in secret hush. Traces of people fade into the darkness, and a solitary figure leaves behind the lingering resonance of a walk home. In a moment where time stands still, within an unbroken scene, that person walks quietly, almost unseen.

도쿄 주오구에서 마주친 거리의 고요한 밤. 신호등이 멀리 있는 명령을 속삭이며 부드러운 침묵을 내뿜는다. 가로등의 점멸하는 빛들이 거리 위에 스며들며. 수많은 발자국들이 지나갔던 이 길 위은, 이제는 텅 비어 잠을 청한다. 그림자가 길게 늘어지고는 밤. 은밀하게 살아있는 도시의 빛들. 사람들의 흔적은 어둠 속으로 사그라들고, 홀로 걷는 이가 집으로 가는 긴 여운을 남긴다. 잠시 멈춰 선 시간 속에서, 깨지지 않은 장면 속에서 그 사람이 살금살금 걷고 있다.

MQMQ+H34, Chuo City, Tokyo, Japan

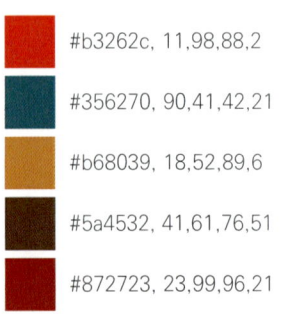

#b3262c, 11,98,88,2
#356270, 90,41,42,21
#b68039, 18,52,89,6
#5a4532, 41,61,76,51
#872723, 23,99,96,21

In a small izakaya in Ueno, as the city's noise gently seeps into the lantern's glow, our evening breathes in warmth for a brief moment. Sake flows, and conversations weave between strangers and friends, threading past and present into countless synopses. This cozy corner, hidden beneath neon lights, holds a thousand whispers in every nook. Here, laughter and sorrow melt into the fabric of time. Life continues endlessly, and our worries never quite cease—how to live, how to endure, how we will be carried along.

우에노의 작은 선술집에서, 도시의 소음이 부드럽게 등불의 빛 속으로 스며들 때, 우리의 저녁은 잠깐동안 따뜻함으로 숨을 쉰다. 사케가 흘러가고, 낯선 이들과 친구들 사이에서 대화가 연결되며, 과거와 현재가 엮여 여러 갈래의 시놉시스를 만든다. 네온 아래 숨겨진 이 작고 안락한 구석은 모퉁이마다 수많은 속삭임을 간직하고 있다. 웃음과 슬픔이 시간 속에서 녹고 있는 곳. 삶은 끊임없이 이어져 우리의 고민은 멈출 줄 모른다. 어떻게 살 것인가, 어떻게 살아낼 것인가, 어떻게 살아질 것인가에 대해.

6 Chome-7-10 Ueno, Taito City, Tokyo 110-0005, Japan

#30689d, 94,51,14,2

#a4cce8, 44,4,4,0

#b78b30, 18,45,96,6

#885e2b, 27,61,96,24

#724323, 30,74,98,37

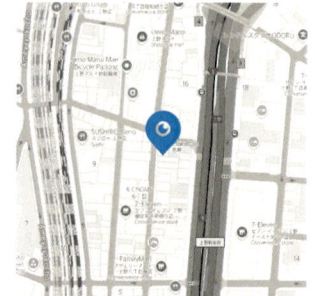

On Dogenzaka street, streetlights flicker softly, showering blessings upon those whose long shadows stretch across the road. The alleys of Shibuya never find time to sleep. They move tirelessly once more, purifying the city that boiled and simmered all day, resetting everything so that by morning, these streets will be pristine again. The pace of downtown gradually slows, and the city's rhythm fades, like music drifting into the distance.

도겐자카 거리의 가로등이 부드럽게 깜박이며 길 위의 긴 그림자를 드리운 사람들에게 축복을 쏟아내는 밤. 시부야의 골목은 잠들 겨를이 없다. 낮 동안 부글대며 끓던 도시를 말끔하게 정화시키기 위해 다시 부지런히 움직인다. 모든 것을 리셋 시켜야 내일 아침 이 골목은 다시 말끔해질 테니. 도심의 속도는 점점 느려지고. 도시의 리듬은 마치 멀어지는 음악처럼 점점 사그라든다.

2 Chome Dogenzaka, Shibuya, Tokyo 150-0043

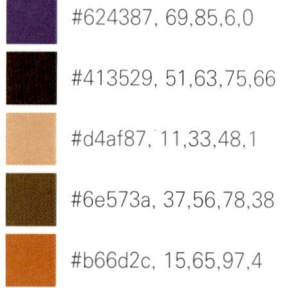

#624387, 69,85,6,0

#413529, 51,63,75,66

#d4af87, 11,33,48,1

#6e573a, 37,56,78,38

#b66d2c, 15,65,97,4

A heart paused at the red signal. Quiet tension seeps into the night air. In the distance, a tower of light pierces the darkness, while blurred footsteps linger at the border between reality and dreams. Warmth escapes from behind windows, spreading across the cold, silent streets. The city's breath continues slowly, small moments of waiting gathering beneath the lights. With every halted moment comes a sense of something about to begin, and in each fading silhouette, a lingering afterglow remains.

붉은 신호에 잠시 멈춘 마음. 밤공기 속에 스며드는 고요한 긴장. 멀리서 번지는 빛의 탑이 어둠을 뚫고 올라가고, 흐릿한 발걸음은 현실과 꿈의 경계에 머문다. 창문 너머로 새어 나오는 온기, 차가운 거리 위로 번지는 적막. 도시의 숨결은 느리게 이어지고, 불빛 아래 쌓여가는 작은 기다림. 멈춰선 순간마다 어딘가로 이어질 듯한 예감, 사라지는 뒷모습에 긴 여운이 남겨진다.

Basement of TOSPA Building, Chuo City, Tokyo, 103-0005, Japan

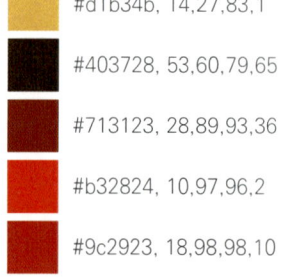

The night on Kiyamachi-dori breathes softly. Neon warmth spreads in the hush of evening, low whispers gathering at the mouth of the alley. The air holds Kyoto's stories: familiar loneliness and fleeting anticipation quietly dissolve into the darkness. Small hopes linger at the fingertips. The city's breath tangles and spreads along the wires, and the day's fatigue seeps into the silence of those who sit. Distant laughter and lights, the lingering traces of passing footsteps. On this night where bustle and stillness cross paths, memories of today slowly settle into the alley, holding the uncertainty of tomorrow. Light gently asks the way, like a memory that will never truly fade.

교야마치 도리의 밤은 부드럽게 숨을 쉰다. 저녁의 적막 속에 번지는 네온의 온기. 골목 어귀에 쌓여가는 낮은 속삭임. 공기는 교토의 이야기를 품고 있고, 익숙한 외로움과 스쳐가는 설렘이 어둠 속에 조용히 녹아든다. 손끝에 머무는 작은 기대. 도시의 숨결이 전선 위로 얽혀 퍼지고, 앉아 있는 이들의 침묵에 하루의 피로가 스며든다. 멀리서 들려오는 웃음과 불빛, 지나가는 발걸음에 남겨진 여운. 분주함과 고요함이 교차하는 밤, 불확실한 내일을 품은 채 오늘의 기억이 천천히 골목에 내려앉는다. 빛은 아련하게 길을 묻는다. 결코 완전히 사라지지 않을 기억처럼.

2Q3C+M6P Kyoto, Japan

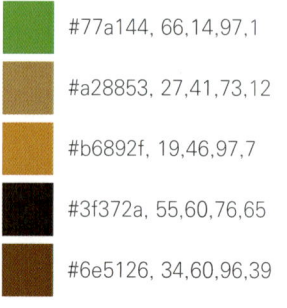

#77a144, 66,14,97,1

#a28853, 27,41,73,12

#b6892f, 19,46,97,7

#3f372a, 55,60,76,65

#6e5126, 34,60,96,39

In the gentle dusk, amber lanterns spill softly onto the street, brushing the silhouettes of people quietly walking toward their destinations. Warmth escapes from behind windows. Fleeting encounters linger on the afterimage of a passing bus. The grain of tranquil time. A lingering trace remains in a gaze that pauses for a moment. Small hopes gather at the corner of the alley. In that evening where darkness and light entwine, deep twilight wraps around the heart, and the day's fatigue slowly melts away in the drifting breeze. Beneath the faintly spreading lights, familiar footsteps cross paths with a quiet anticipation for somewhere unknown. Within the streets of Nara, the journey and each moment rest quietly, whispering softly like a lyrical poem.

부드러운 해질녘, 호박색 등불이 거리로 부드럽게 쏟아져 나와, 목적지를 향해 조용히 걷는 사람들의 실루엣을 살며시 스친다. 창 너머로 새어 나오는 온기. 지나가는 버스의 잔상에 얹힌 짧은 인연. 고요한 시간의 결. 잠시 머무는 시선 속에 남겨지는 여운. 골목 어귀에 쌓여가는 작은 기대. 어둠과 빛이 어우러진 그 저녁에, 짙은 저녁빛이 마음을 감싸고, 스치는 바람에 하루의 피로가 천천히 녹아내린다. 희미하게 번지는 불빛 아래, 익숙한 발걸음과 어딘가로 향하는 설렘이 교차하고. 나라의 거리 속에 고요히 깃든 여정과 순간을 서정적인 시처럼 낮게 속삭인다.

MRMQ+CR7 Nara, Japan

#9f6e31, 23,57,93,14

#cf972e, 9,44,96,1

#e7c72a, 6,18,96,0

#303b6d, 96,87,23,11

#333156, 91,91,33,28

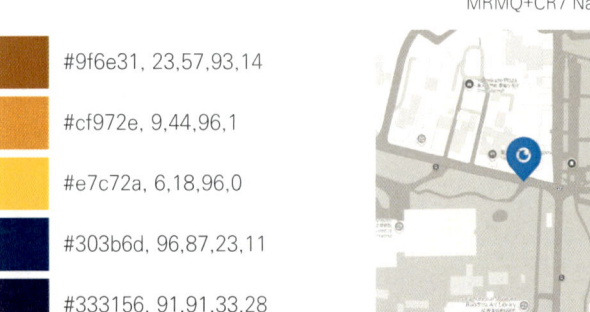

In the moment where pause and flow intersect, the warmth of night seeps into a corner of the heart. Between spreading lights and fleeting speed, silent waiting lingers at the ear. The grain of time passes over cracked crosswalks, silhouettes brushing by like the wind. Unfamiliar excitement and the city's quiet breath drift through familiar scenery. Gazes pause beneath the red signal, while shadows slip carelessly across striped lines. In a brief, ringing moment, at the crossroads where darkness and light entwine, today's strange memories slowly take root.

멈춤과 흐름이 교차하는 순간, 마음 한 켠에 밤의 온기가 스며든다. 번지는 불빛과 스치는 속도 사이, 말 없는 기다림이 귓가에 머문다. 균열진 횡단보도 위로 지나가는 시간의 결. 바람처럼 스쳐가는 뒷모습. 익숙한 풍경 속에 남겨진 낯선 설렘도, 도시의 숨결도 조용히 번진다. 붉은 신호 아래 시선들은 잠시 멈추고. 그림자들은 무심한 스트라이프 위로 흘러간다. 마음이 잠시 쨍하고 번지는 순간, 어둠과 빛이 교차하는 교차로에서 오늘의 생경한 기억이 천천히 깃든다.

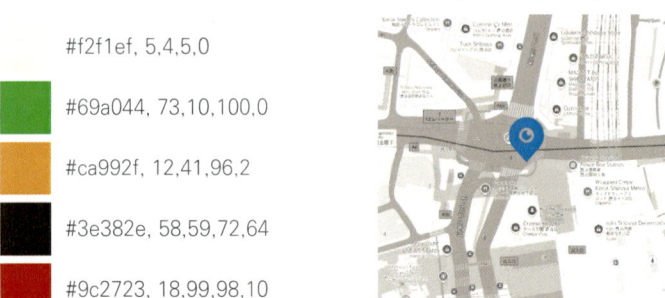

MP52+Q73 Shibuya, Tokyo, Japan

#f2f1ef, 5,4,5,0

#69a044, 73,10,100,0

#ca992f, 12,41,96,2

#3e382e, 58,59,72,64

#9c2723, 18,99,98,10

The gossipy whispers of neon lights. Trains rush by, ears closed, as fleeting as a single moment. Reflected light gently caresses the cold concrete. People cross the streets in synchronized steps, moving to the city's vast rhythm. The city quietly carries the threads of their lives. In the alleys of Taito, the air murmurs with tangled stories, and Tokyo's light becomes a secret shared only at night. Here, past and present, stillness and bustle, life and a certain death quietly meet beneath the glow of streetlamps, willingly bearing the breath of the city.

네온 불빛의 수다스러운 속삭임. 기차는 귀를 막은 채, 한 순간처럼 빠르게 지나가고. 반사된 빛은 차가운 콘크리트를 부드럽게 어루만진다. 사람들은 거대한 리듬 속에서 동기화된 걸음으로 거리를 가로지르고. 도시는 그들의 삶을 묵묵히 이어준다. 타이토의 골목. 여러 갈래의 이야기를 속삭이는 공기 속에서 도쿄의 그 빛은 밤에만 나누는 비밀이다. 여기, 과거와 현재, 조용함과 사글벅적함, 삶과 어떤 죽음이 가로등 불빛 속에서 조용히 조우하며, 도시의 숨결을 기꺼이 감당한다.

PQ6G+F37 Taito City, Tokyo, Japan

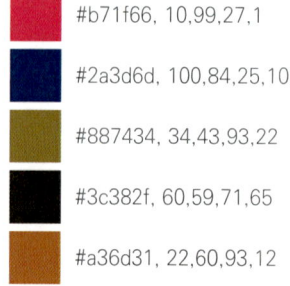

#b71f66, 10,99,27,1
#2a3d6d, 100,84,25,10
#887434, 34,43,93,22
#3c382f, 60,59,71,65
#a36d31, 22,60,93,12

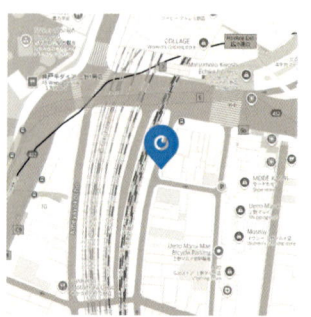

Honmachi, Semba Center Building, Hall 10, first floor. The corridor unfolds quietly, as if linking past and present. Evening light spills across the floor. Elongated shadows whisper forgotten stories. The space remains in its purest form, stripped of unnecessary ornament, speaking of both the moment and eternity at once. With each step, the silence deepens. The passageway imprints the presence of those who have passed through. In this minimalist corridor, time bends softly, saturating the air with its gentle presence.

혼마치 센바센터빌딩 10호관 1층. 그 통로는 마치 과거와 현재가 잇고 있는 듯 고요하게 펼쳐진다. 저녁의 빛이 바닥에 흐르고. 길게 드리운 그림자는 잊혀진 이야기를 속삭인다. 불필요한 장식 없이 본연의 형태로만 남은 공간. 순간과 영원을 동시에 이야기한다. 걸음마다 고요는 깊어지고. 통로는 지나간 이들의 존재를 공간에 각인한다. 이 미니멀한 통로 속에서 시간은 부드럽게 휘어지면서 공기 속에 잔뜩 스며들어 있다.

3 Chome Senbachūō, Chuo Ward, Osaka, 541-0055, Japan

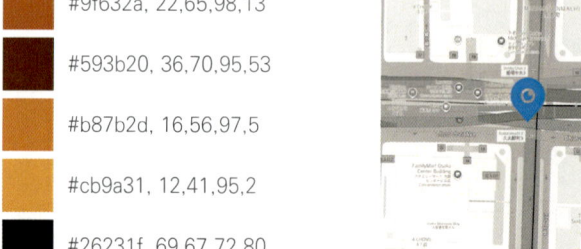

#9f632a, 22,65,98,13

#593b20, 36,70,95,53

#b87b2d, 16,56,97,5

#cb9a31, 12,41,95,2

#26231f, 69,67,72,80

The canal of Dotonbori. Neon waves soak the heart, and the whispers of night ripple across the water. Laughter and anticipation of people seep into the darkness, and flowing time shimmers with brilliance. A familiar strangeness, a moment where excitement and freedom intertwine. Shards of light scatter across the surface, while the city's heart beats quietly. A longing spirit drifts somewhere, leaving a lingering trace in the fading noise. Emotions brush by like the wind, warmth lingers in a gaze paused for a moment. The night's temperature and the texture of light blend together, and everything continues to flow as if in a gentle current.

도톤보리의 수로. 네온의 파도가 마음을 적시고, 밤의 속삭임이 물결 위로 번진다. 사람들의 웃음과 기대가 어둠에 스며들고, 흐르는 시간은 반짝임으로 가득하다. 익숙한 낯섦, 설렘과 자유가 교차하는 순간. 빛의 조각들이 물 위에 흩어지며, 도시의 심장은 조용히 뛰고 있다. 어딘가로 떠나는 마음, 멀어지는 소음 속에 남겨진 여운. 바람처럼 스치는 감정, 잠시 멈춘 시선 속에 머무는 온기. 밤의 온도와 빛의 결이 어우러진 채, 모든 것이 흐르듯 이어진다.

MG93+JMP Osaka, Japan

#b32426, 10,99,94,2
#36343c, 74,70,53,57
#434486, 87,83,8,1
#d0b32e, 14,25,97,1
#886a2d, 31,50,96,24

A dark corner in an Osaka alley. Neon lights slice through the night, flickering like whispers of forgotten desires. A solitary figure drifts within, becoming the city's pulse. The electronic hum of the streets and fading old tales are fleeting illusions, trapped between echoes. Neon signs reflect in her eyes, yet there is no warmth within them—only the cold promise of passing moments. What stories were exchanged here? What sorrow lurks in the shadows? Beneath the flashing advertisements, memories tangled among countless names cross and recross like electric wires in the night.

오사카의 어두운 골목 모퉁이. 네온 불빛이 밤을 가르며 잊혀진 욕망들의 속삭임처럼 깜빡인다. 그 속을 떠도는 한 사람은 도시의 맥박이 되어. 거리의 전자음과 사라져가는 오래된 이야기들은 메아리 사이에 갇힌 일시적인 환상이다. 네온 사인의 빛이 그녀의 눈 속에 투영되지만, 그 눈동자속엔 따뜻함이 없다. 스쳐 지나가는 순간들의 차가운 약속만이 있을 뿐. 어떤 이야기들이 오갔나. 어떤 슬픔이 도사리고 있는가. 번쩍이는 광고들 아래, 숱한 이름들 속에 얽힌 기억이 전깃줄처럼 복잡하게 교차하는 밤.

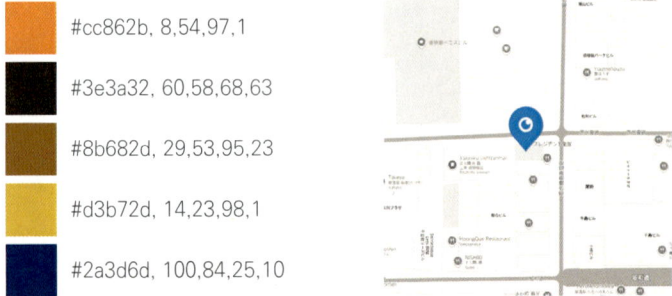

1-chōme-7 Sennichimae, Chuo Ward, Osaka, 542-0074, Japan

#cc862b, 8,54,97,1
#3e3a32, 60,58,68,63
#8b682d, 29,53,95,23
#d3b72d, 14,23,98,1
#2a3d6d, 100,84,25,10

A strange longing seeps into the entrance of an alley at Sennichimae. Neon lights flicker faintly, like a forgotten melody. Beneath the red lanterns of a yakiniku shop, a lonely warmth spreads. Whispers blend with the night air, and a quiet anticipation gently soaks the heart. Within the alley, the slow grain of time and a hush that lingers like old memories fill the space. Silent solitude and familiar comfort cross paths, and yet another day leaves its traces in the alley. A lingering afterglow remains in a corner of the heart. And still, beneath the lights, small hopes quietly gather.

낯선 그리움이 센니치마에 골목 어귀에 스며들고. 네온 불빛은 잊혀진 멜로디처럼 아련히 깜빡인다. 야끼니꾸 가게의 붉은 등불 아래 쓸쓸한 온기가 번진다. 속삭임이 밤공기와 뒤섞여, 조용한 설렘이 마음을 적신다. 골목 안에는 느릿한 시간의 결과 오래된 추억처럼 머무는 정적이 가득하다. 고요한 외로움과 익숙한 위로가 교차하고, 또 하나의 하루는 골목 속에 잔상으로 밴다. 한다. 마음 한 귀퉁이에 남는 아련한 여운. 그러나 불빛 아래 쌓여가는 작은 희망.

1-chōme-7 Sennichimae, Chuo Ward, Osaka, 542-0074, Japan

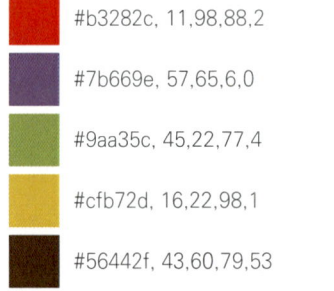

A gentle warmth spreads through the evening air, old memories seeping into a quiet corner of the heart. Under the faint glow of lights, small happiness gathers. Soft laughter and whispers tenderly brush the soul. Time flows slowly yet densely, familiar longing stretching all the way to the end of the alley. In the moment where darkness and light cross paths, forgotten excitement quietly blooms. Every passing step leaves a lingering trace, and tiny hopes shimmer beneath the lights. At the edge of an ordinary day, the heart pauses for a moment, embracing its warmest memories.

저녁 공기 속에 번지는 따스한 온기, 오래된 추억이 가슴 한켠에 스며든다. 희미한 불빛 아래 쌓여가는 소소한 행복. 조용한 웃음과 속삭임이 마음을 어루만진다. 느리지만 조밀하게 흐르는 시간, 익숙한 그리움이 골목 끝까지 이어진다. 어둠과 빛이 교차하는 순간, 잊고 있던 설렘이 조용히 피어난다. 지나가는 발걸음마다 남겨지는 여운, 작은 희망이 불빛 아래에서 반짝인다. 평범한 하루의 끝자락에서, 마음은 잠시 멈춰 서서 따뜻한 기억을 안는다.

MRMR+F2C Nara, Japan

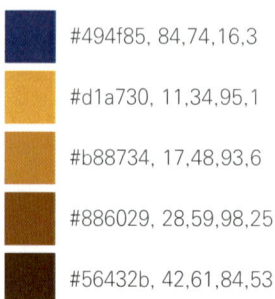

#494f85, 84,74,16,3
#d1a730, 11,34,95,1
#b88734, 17,48,93,6
#886029, 28,59,98,25
#56432b, 42,61,84,53

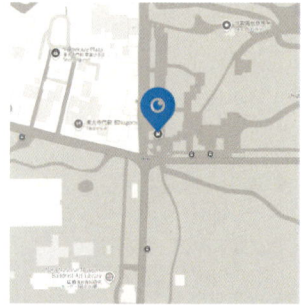

Evening light of Kyoto cradles the narrow alley, as the sound of bicycle wheels scatters across the rain-kissed cobblestones. A night imbued with tranquil breaths. The wheels glide like whispers over glistening stone. Beneath faint lanterns, murmurs soak into the dusk, while above, tangled wires scribble emotions across the violet sky. Time drifts slowly. The wind returns, laced with the scent of memory. The lights shimmer with a human warmth, and shadows quietly embrace each other. Longing lingers on the path, floating between stillness and sentiment.

교토의 저녁빛이 골목을 감싸 안고, 자전거 바퀴 소리가 젖은 돌길 위로 번진다. 고요한 숨결을 담은 밤. 자전거 바퀴가 젖은 돌길 위를 미끄러지듯 지나간다. 희미한 등불 아래 어스름한 속삭임들이 스며들고, 퍼플빛 하늘엔 낡은 전깃줄이 엉킨 감정처럼 어지럽다. 시간은 느릿하게 흐른다. 추억의 냄새를 품고 돌아드는 바람. 불빛은 사람의 온기를 닮아 반짝거리며, 그림자들은 말없이 서로를 감싸안는다. 어딘가 그리운 마음들이 길 위에 남아, 정적과 감성 사이를 유영한다.

2Q4C+464 Kyoto, Japan

#6f4424, 31,72,96,39
#9f642b, 22,64,97,13
#cc852e, 8,55,95,1
#cf952d, 9,45,96,1
#3b3755, 84,83,36,31

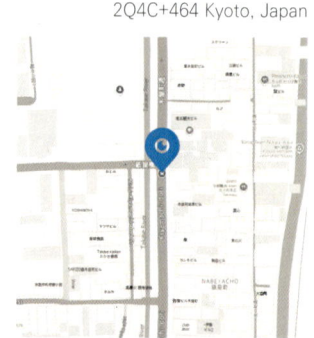

Across the Takase River, caf windows quietly reflect the gentle light of a city at rest. Inside, the sound of conversation shimmers like calm water, its warmth carried across the river. Each window holds moments unfolding—laughter, whispered stories, the joy of being together. The flowing river silently witnesses their lives as they open, and as night deepens, the heart of Kyoto beats softly within the embrace of the caf .

다카세 강 건너, 카페 창문은 고요히 휴식 중인 도시의 부드러운 빛을 반사한다. 그 안에서 대화의 소리는 조용한 강물처럼 일렁이며, 그 따스함은 강을 넘어 전해진다. 각 창문마다 이어지는 순간들이 담겨 있다. 웃음, 소곤소곤 나누는 이야기들, 함께 있다는 기쁨. 흐르는 강물이 그들의 펼쳐지는 삶들을 잠잠히 지켜보고, 밤이 깊어갈수록 교토의 심장은 카페의 품에서 조용히 울린다.

2Q3C+Q6P Kyoto, Japan

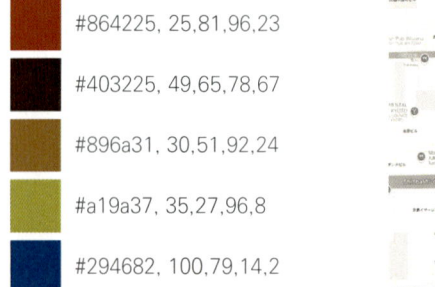

#864225, 25,81,96,23
#403225, 49,65,78,67
#896a31, 30,51,92,24
#a19a37, 35,27,96,8
#294682, 100,79,14,2